UWot?!

**what those text
messages *really* mean**

Stuart McLean

SUMMERSDALE

Summersdale Publishers Ltd
46 West Street
Chichester
PO19 1RP   UK

www.summersdale.com

ISBN 1 84024 215 9

Printed and bound in Great Britain.

Introduction

Whoever said, 'The art of communication is dead,' had obviously never sent an email or used a mobile phone.

Not only is communication alive and well, but with the text message it has truly entered the twenty-first century. Sending text is slick, fast, efficient, concise and very minimalist.

There's no better way to say exactly what you want because it hides that embarrassing blush as you tell a little white lie, and the guilty look in your eyes when you tell a whopping great howler. What's more, you can simply ignore any irate replies and best of all there's absolutely no chance of getting a slap in the face. But remember, it works both ways! So be wise and bear all this in mind when *reading* messages.

This little book of text will not only ensure you never fall foul of a cryptic message, it will guarantee that you become a master of this growing art form.

♂2♀

ILuvU

I'm in bed with your best friend.

SxWasGREAT-IlCalU2Mrow

There's more chance of there being intelligent asparagus living on Mars than there is of my calling you.

CUSoon

Have dropped into the pub for a few drinks and will crawl home in a drunken stupor in about six hours. So get ready for some wild passionate sex.

HdSmlXident-DntWryImOK

> I cut off my left arm with a chainsaw and have been rushed into intensive care where I am awaiting extensive microsurgery.

MsingU-Lukin4Wrd2UCuminHome!

> Fridge empty! Pile of dishes in sink! No sex for a week! I can't cope without you!

ILuvUandSoDoI

> I may be schizophrenic but at least we like you.

HdOwsumTmeLstNite-RSVP-PLEASE

What a night! Don't remember a thing – but some chick penned her mobile number across my chest! I wonder what she looks like?

PlsePlseMarryMe

I know I should have told you this sooner as you're getting married to someone else in an hour but it's only fair that I let you know that I have always loved you and can't contemplate life without you.

LtsSpndaRmnticNiteHmeAlon

Cancel our plans for a night on the
town. I lost all my wages on a
'dead cert' so we'll have to stay
home and watch TV instead.

SryCntCalU-Im@MprtntMtng

I have taken the afternoon off and
am currently undertaking an
important putt at the sixteenth.

urXed

Darling, I am sorry to have to
break this sad news to you, but last
night I met the most wonderful,
intelligent, beautiful girl. I think
I've fallen in love with her and so

I'm devastated to have to tell you that our relationship does not appear to have much of a future.

LtsJstXAndMakUp

Macho Law forbids me from ever admitting I'm wrong. However, I would like us to end our week-long argument now and for you to iron my shirt.

BotUaBigBnchOf @>—:—

Yes, I am guilty of whatever you accuse me of (and probably more)!

what those text messages *really* mean

URMy1+Only

My other two girlfriends have just dumped me.

IvRangdARmantcEvning4OurAnivrsry

Burgers and coke, a scary movie then back to my place for a quick shag – you can't get more romantic than that.

YNotInvitUrMumRnd2Nite?

You can do what the hell you like – I'm going out with my mates.

DoUFncyGoinOnHols2gthr?

> I want to take you away for a dirty weekend.

LstNiteULukd$1000000

> I love it when you dress like a slut.

MetUrM8LstNite-ShesHOT

> I have a moronic lack of understanding about women and am destined for a life of misery.

ThnkinAbtU

> I'm masturbating.

ILLLLLLLLLIKEU

No matter how hard I try, the LOVE word is just impossible to say.

SryWhtDidUSayInLstMssage?

Not only do I never listen to you; I seldom bother to read your messages either.

LtsMkeMadPason8Luv

I'm feeling horny and fancy some wild erotic sex – do you have four minutes to spare?

OfCorsIRspectU

Sure I respect you . . . now get your kit off.

ImHppy4U2HavSxWthOthrs

How about arranging a threesome with your best mate?

IThnkImDYING

I may be a hypochondriac – but it's only when I'm feeling sick.

IWudLuv2SpndAlDayShopngWthU

Love makes me do some nice things. It also makes me do some bloody stupid things.

ImACarinSnsitvePrson

> Actually I don't give a damn about anyone except myself.

WIBL8-DamCarBrknDwn

> Have been driving around in circles for ages, trying to find the restaurant. However, I don't need to ask directions as I drive on sheer instinct and male cunning.

Wnted2TelUThtIRelyThnkURGorgus &WldLuv2GetIntim8WthUBtIWas2 Shy2TelUFace2Face

> This little message always does the trick – she'll fall straight into my little trap.

UWot?!

LtsEnjoyThsSpcalFrndshp
UnitdinCmpleteKndnes

> Hope this subliminal message
> does the trick!

SzeDsntMater

> Your tits are much too small but
> don't worry – for your birthday
> I've got you a Wonderbra.

IvGotAHedak

> I'm sorry sex only lasted three
> minutes. Did you achieve orgasm?

♀2♂

ICntCU2NiteIHve02Wear

I've tried on thirty-two of my outfits but none of them are quite right today. It's time for some serious shopping.

GotAPrOfShoes@Sales

Actually I bought eight pairs – none of them fit but they're all gorgeous.

AFAIC-MarriageIsNAGI

As far as I'm concerned, marriage is not only a good idea it's my only idea! It fills my every thought and all my dreams – so why, why, why won't you propose?

DoNOT-TMB!

Don't dare text me back. I demand the last word! Always!

GOOML SCUMBAG

You forgot to send me a Valentine's day card.

Cum2MyFlatL8r PS-IDoNOTUslyDoThis!

I'm a nymphomaniac.

FckOffUBstrd

I love you dearly but it's the wrong time of the month.

ILuvUXactlyAsUR

Rude! Arrogant! Inconsiderate! Time for a change!

CU2Nite@8

Confirming our dinner date for this evening; get there by eight. I'll turn up around nine without even a word of apology.

UNvrLsten2ME

I want to share everything with you, my every thought, my joys, my achievements, my tears, my sorrows. Why oh why are you so inconsiderate and disinterested when I'm opening up my heart to you and pouring out my soul in minute detail? It seems to me that the more I try to tell you the less willing you are to listen.

IlBRdyIn5Mins

Have to have a shower, choose an outfit, phone my best friend and put on my makeup – shouldn't take too long!

URInMyEvryThotSnceWeMet

Since we met I can't get you out of my head. I think about you constantly. I just can't remember whether you were drop-dead gorgeous or whether I was just completely pissed!

CumHomSoonDearestDarling

If you're not back here in twenty minutes I'm moving out, you good-for-nothing swine.

Hlp!EmrgncyHuryHomeQck

Aaaaaargh! There's a spider in the bath!

WeNd2Tlk

It's been quite a while since we
last had a fight.

=O=

Buy me a diamond ring or get out
of my life!

ImHppy4U2COthrGrls

Die you bastard!

UDntHve2ByMeABrthdyPressie

If you have a death wish that is.

MyCrditCrdWntWrk!

I'm on a massive spending spree but suddenly shops won't accept my card – why's that?

IvStrtedDecor8ngThHouse

I've done the hard bit – buying the wallpaper and paint – you can do the rest.

ImRlyInThMood4SumSensulPlesur

I'm desperate for some chocolate.

ITrstUCmpltly

Hopefully you'll now feel too guilty to misbehave.

UCnTrstMeCmpltly

> I'm careful and discreet.

URMyMrRIGHT

> Mega-rich! Eighty! Heart
> condition! Perfect!

I4GiveU

> Now that I've cut all your clothes
> in half I'm willing to consider
> reconciliation.

SzeDsntMater

> Your penis is much too small but
> don't worry – a recent survey
> showed that sexual pleasure is not

dependent on size. Of course, many women may find this hard to swallow.

IvGotAHedak

Don't even look at me!

♀2♀

ImGoin2GoCasual2Prty

You're going to be *so* jealous when you see the sexy new designer outfit I've bought for tonight's party.

TBH-Im2Bzy2Go2Clb2Nite

To be honest, now that I've hit thirty, I'm just too tired to go clubbing after a hard day's work.

UlookGr8InUrNuDress

God, your bum looks big in that!

HavngaBHD

I *was* having a Bad Hair Day! So I comforted myself by visiting my stylist, beautician and fashion designer.

URMyNo1FRIEND

I'm feeling guilty because I've been gossiping about you behind your back. Thought I should remind you that we're best friends – just in case you find out what I said.

FixtUaD8WthGr8SxyHUNK

My boyfriend has a really geeky mate who's every bit as desperate as you.

UCnBoroMyClthsNEtimeULke

I need to borrow your new dress for a party next week.

IvMetAGr8SnsitveRspctableGuy

Actually he's a gun-carrying, drug-dealing Mafia hit-man – but he's so cute.

ImInLuv

I desperately need to be in love. So I've attached myself to the nearest guy.

IH8U-IH8U-IH8U-IH8U

April Fool! Oh! How many days *are* there in March?

what those text messages *really* mean

U - - - SLUT - - - ME

Just between you and me I think she's a real slut.

DuYaTkinhIvHad3Mcuh5Drink

I'm totally pissed.

IvStrtedANewDiet

Straight after this cream cake and box of sweets I'm going to give some serious thought to going on a diet.

thBUMis

Does my bum look big in this?

IvGtAScret2TelU-
PromisNt2TelASoul

> Here's a juicy bit of gossip but
> don't pass it on until I've finished
> telling all my friends.

♂2♂

FncyAQckBeer?

Let's spend the whole night at the pub and only leave when we feel compelled to consume a greasy doner kebab.

3-0ItsJstEEzy

We're three-nil up – it's just too easy.

1-0?

Have you scored with that new chick yet?

CntGo2Pub-ImGoin2Gym2WrkOut

I don't dare admit that I'm staying home to watch my favourite soap on television.

IDntFUrCk

I don't fancy your chick and I'm not too impressed with mine either. Let's make an excuse and get out of here.

ImInLuv

Hey, have you seen Jennifer Aniston in her new movie?

MyMsPrfectWudBSnsitve+Carin

Provided, of course, she had huge
boobs and a cute bum.

YAWANAGO2OPERA?

Fooled you mate – I've got the
Cup Final tickets.

ISpntThHoleDayShopng

I went to the supermarket and got
a six-month supply of booze.

SheLuksSXY

Isn't it a really weird phenomenon
– after 2 a.m. nobody's ugly?

FncyAFewBrs?

Beers? Bears? Bares? I don't mind; you choose.

IDntGveAShitAbotEneone

Actually I'm a caring, sensitive person.

Luv Xchange

HowRU?

Shit, it's been days since I've been in touch I hope she's not mad.

ImOK&U?

Swine, he's ignored me for weeks.

AbFab

Well – apart from the hangover.

Luv2CU

The sooner I tell him I'm dating his mate the quicker I'll get over this guilty feeling.

UWot?!

Gr8-ASAP

Phew! She's not mad with me.

2Nite?

Better get this over with.

SryNeed2Wrk2Nite

Hell. Not tonight I've got a red-hot date.

Soon?

The swine – how dare he turn me down?

VrySOON

Yippee – I'm dating two chicks at the same time.

Martian and Vesuvian Textual Intercourse

&*£@((=+%!!*

> We have come to Venus to destroy your planet.

diuhzmodsrcrapiheuhiuhefiuheuihiuew

> Thanks – mine's a gin and tonic.

^"^%"£"$"£%£^^%%^

> Sexy? Me? You think I've got a cute bum?

ytdytuhghalbsrcoolesesrbuuiyufytfyf

> No, Sagittarius actually.

**(*%£"$%£")(%$%$

    I must now impregnate you and
    your friends to ensure the
    continuance of my species.

uirhreiugresmmllmiurhilurewiwuuieiufiu

    Oooo – yes I would love to marry
    you!

$£%%$^$£$£%$%&^%

    You and I seem to speak the same
    language, I insist you come back
    to Mars with me.

FromMe2U

F2T?

If you are free to talk, like a real human being, then call me now. Otherwise we can just continue wasting our time sending moronic, meaningless text messages.

4kOff

I would be very much obliged if you would please go away.

2MorePints&aG&T

Barman, we are much too lazy to walk all the way to the bar, so can you please bring drinks to our table.

UWot?!

Testing 1 2 3 4 5 Testing 1 2 3 4 5
Testing 1 2 3 4 5

> I'm a sad prat with a brand new phone and nothing to say.

DntTxtMe-IlTxtU

> Get lost moron.

.._. .._ _._. _._. — .._. .._..

> I'm a conventionalist so I much prefer to send text in the old-fashioned way.

ThsIsAStckUpHndOvrThe$$$$

Excuse me but I wish to rob this
bank and would be delighted if
you would put lots of money into
this sack marked 'swag'.

HpyBday2U

I'm too damn mean to send a card
so this stupid little message will
just have to do.

(H)~ (A)~ (P)~ (P)~ (Y)~ (B)~ (I)~
(R)~ (T)~ (H)~ (D)~ (A)~ (Y)~

I may be mean but at least I'm
inventive.

zzzzZZZZ

> Your messages are so incredibly boring I've fallen asleep.

χ δ κ μ λ μ δ β φ κ γ η ι

> I shouldn't have bought this bloody stupid phone from that dodgy market trader.

WherRU?

> I haven't the foggiest idea where I am.

$%fZx&M*=O=RjD£

> Bloody cat won't stop playing with the phone.

FUKFFO
> I'm dyslexic.

QQQQQ
> I'm stuck in a long, long queue.

GoDirect2Jail
> Playing Monopoly by text
> message was a pretty dumb idea.

* * * * * *
> It's snowing.

" " " " " "
> It's raining.

" " *CAT* " " *DOG* " "

It's raining cats and dogs.

>>>>>G>>>>>A>>>L>>E

It's blowing a gale.

/\/_/\/_/\/_/\/_ _ _ _ _ _ _ _

My mobile doubles as a heart rate
monitor – I seem to have just
passed away.

_____/_____/_____/_____/_____

You have just taken part in the first
ever mobile Mexican Wave.

IDotADold

> I seem to have suddenly come
> down with a very bad cold.

UR-BpaUinT

> You are a pain in the butt.

PetrPiprPckdAPeckOfPckledPpers
DidPetrPperPckAPeckOfPckledPpers?
IfPetrPiprPckdAPeckOfPckledPpers
WhrsThPeckOfPckledPpersPetrPiprPcked?

> Try this one after six pints!

IleveAlMyStuf2U

This is my Last Will and Testament. Being of totally unsound mind I am leaving everything to you.

" "

You have left me speechless.

Generation Gap

Ooops-BmpdDadsCar-SmlDent-ShudFxOK

After a 100mph motorway chase I crashed Dad's car through the safety barriers. After spinning three times we finally came to rest upside down in a ditch. The good news is I've salvaged the steering wheel.

DntWury

Something AWFUL has happened.

DAD - URGENT - Snd££££Pls

How am I supposed to survive?
It's been days since you sent the
last cheque.

YES MUM- IlBHmeB410

Of course I'll be home before ten
– ten in the morning.

XamWsHARD

I've just flunked my finals.

XamWsEASY

I've just flunked my finals.

MssdLstBus–
Need2StaAtFrndsHwse2Nite

Met a great guy at a rock concert –
he's the lead singer in the band.
We're going back to his hotel
room to chill out.

ImOldEnuf2KnoWhtImDoin

For Pete's sake Mum, stop
interfering and let me live my own
life – after all I'm eleven and
three-quarters.

CumNOW

My dearest darling Dad, I am just
about ready to leave my friend's
house and return home. I would be

delighted if you would be kind
enough to make the twelve-mile
drive through this raging blizzard
to collect me and return me safely
home. I will be forever indebted to
you. Your loving daughter.

HveMetARlyNceGrl-DadWilLuvHr

I'm dating a stripper who works at
the Pink Flamingo Club, she says
she knows Dad really well.

CnIHveAFwM8sRndWhilUrAway?

I've organised a party for all my
friends, and their friends and their
friends and some completely
random strangers. Are the house
contents insured?

Tnks4ThLuvlyBrthdyPressie

Stupid old fart – what am I supposed to do with a hand-knitted, vomit-green jumper that's six sizes too big?

Pickup Lines

IveLstMyPhnNo–CnIHveUrs?
> I am a complete prat.

**ImNewInTwn–
CnIHveDrctns2UrHwse?**
> I am a complete prat.

4Th1stTimeIBlveInLuv@1stSite
> I am a complete prat.

WilluuuuuuuuuuCcccMe222222nite
> I am a complete prat with a very
> bad stutter.

CumBck2MyPad2CMyEtchings

> I am a rather sad and pathetic individual who does indeed have a very large collection of etchings. I would be delighted to bore you with them even though you'd much rather shag.

HeyBigBoyThsIsUrLckyNite-UvSCORED

> I'm a transvestite.

CnIFlrtWthUSxy?

> I'm a married woman with four kids – do you care?

HiSxyULukSoCuteButImGay

This club's so dark I can barely
see what I'm typing. Hope that
sexy chick can understand my
message.

WldULik2DnceOrShalWeGoStr82BED?

I'm so absolutely desperate I
would even consider having sex
with you.

) SEXY ((ME)

If I said you had a sexy body
would you hold it against me?

(U)) ME (

> If I said you had a really fat
> grotesque body would you bugger
> off and leave me alone?

) SEXY ((U)

> If I said that I had a sexy body
> would you realise that I'm an
> arrogant, self-centred egotist?

CH4 CH5 CH3 CH4

> This TV remote control is bloody
> useless.

Knt1Prl1Knt2Prl3Knt1Prl1

> Here's the eightieth instalment of
> the pattern for your cardigan. Will
> send more tomorrow.

OldieText

LtsDoIt69Styl2Nite
> Just for a change let's sleep at
> opposite ends of the bed tonight.

BleveItOrNtIm80+StllAVrgin!
> Yes, my face has looked this way
> since I was sixteen.

IfISedUHdAButiflBdy
WudUHldItAgnstMe?
> If I said you had a beautiful body
> would you fall off your Zimmer?

Im69UNo

Actually I'm 84 ½ but I could pass for 83.

JstWntd2LetUNoThat . . .

Senile dementia is a terrible thing . . . now why am I holding this phone?

LtsPaintThTwnRED2Nite

How about we go to the bingo tonight?

IvStilGotAlMyOwnHairUNo

I keep it in a little box on the dressing-table for sentimental reasons.

IStilLeadAnActveSxLfe

I think about sex four times a
week and get an erection twice a
week – not at the same time of
course.

Obtuse Abuse

what those text messages *really* mean

UrLitesROnBtNobdysHome

UHveThWitOfARttn2mato

URAFuClnsShrtOfACrcus

URAFuFrysShrtOfAHppyMeal

UDntHavAlUrCrnflksIn1Box

UrWheelIsSpningBtThHmstrsDEAD

UWot?!

URAFuFethrsShrtOfaDuk

URAFuCrckrsShrtOfaPckt

UHveAnIntelctRyvldOnlyByGrdnTools

UrLevtorDsntGoAlThWay2ThTopFloor

UrMsingAFuBttonsOnUrRmoteCntrl

Instant Insults

	UWot?!
:)	You look like a frog.
:(	You look like a sad frog.
uW//	You are a total wanker.
:-(—0‹	Yes, your bum *does* look big in that.
).(—› (.)	I see the diet's not working.
IQ‹B	Your IQ is less than a bee's.

I8U I hate you.

I9U I used to hate you but now I absolutely detest you.

URNotYY You're not too wise.

U0.5Wit You are a half-wit.

Ear 0 Ear You've got nothing between the ears.

;-)}} You're getting a double chin.

UWot?!	

\(:-(You're going bald.

{:-)   I suspect you're wearing a toupee.

}:-(After that slight updraft I now know that you're wearing a toupee.

Arsicons

(PA . IN)

You are a pain in the arse.

(QE2)

You're a royal pain in the arse.

(_._)

You have a big arse.

(!)

You are a tight arse.

(_?_)

You are a dumb arse.

(_E=mc² _)

You are a smart arse.

(_13_)

You are an unlucky arse.

(~)

You are a sweaty arse.

(_x_)

You can kiss my arse.

(_X_)

Leave my arse alone.

(_magnet_)

I find your arse strangely attractive.

Titicons

(O O)

I have huge tits.

(o o)

I have tiny tits.

(6 6)

I have huge droopy tits.

(Q Q)

I have nipple rings.

(£ £)

I am a lap dancer.

(A D)

I have very lopsided tits.

(@ @)

I never wear a bra when jogging.

(♣ ♣)

You may have noticed – I'm a bit different from other girls.

(\O O/)

I love my Wonderbra.

(* */)

My Wonderbra doesn't work!

(* *)

I am a guy.

Getting Down
to Romance

+Y+Y+Y YES PLSE IlMryU

Of course I would love to marry you. (Who is this message from? Never mind – I'm so desperate I'll marry anyone.)

heUart

You are forever in my heart. (Like a big nagging Ulcer!)

<———— LOVE ————>

I love you this much. (I like to spread my love around.)

ABCDEFGHIUJKL

In my alphabet You and I will always be together. (I'm totally dyslexic.)

F-T-RE

> My future has no meaning without you. (You do not feature in my future.)

_/\/_/\/_/\/_/\/_ _ _ _ _/\/
_/\/_/\/\ _

> My heart skips a beat every time I see you. (Particularly when I'm with another guy!)

— ME —U —>

> I've just been struck by Cupid's arrow. (I wish Robin Hood would practice elsewhere!)

U♥4Ever

I have given you my heart for all eternity. (I've just found the heart symbol on my telephone.)

9 12, 15, 21, 5 23, 15, 21

It's no enigma – I love you. (If I give you my bank account number will you leave me alone?)

LIovUe

I am in love with you. (I am in love. You are in love. Luckily not with each other.)

YMOEU

> I love to feel You wrapped all around Me. (You are smothering me.)

U - - SAD - - ME

> When Me and You are apart I feel so sad. (You are sad so stay away from Me.)

Instant
Philosophy

UWot?!

EvrySlvrLningHsACloud

ThErlyBrdGtsThWrmBt
Th2ndMowsGtsThChees

GodGveManABrainAndAPnis
BtOnlyEnufBlud2Opr81@ATme

RmembrUrUniqJstLikEvryoneEls

TimeIsThBstTcherUnfrtn8ly
ItKilsAlItsStudnts

CndomsREsier2ChngThanNppys

what those text messages *really* mean

YstrdyINuNthng2dayIKnoThat

EvrythngIsSumwhre

AllGenrliz8onsRFlse

GveMeAmbgutyOrGveMeSmethngEls

NoMtterWherUGoUrTher

AbndnThSrch4Truth-Sttle4AGudFntasy

UWot?!

ConscusnesIsThtAnoyngTmeBtweenNaps

HeWhoLafsLstThnksSlowst

IDntSffrFrmInsnityINjoyEvryMnuteOfIt

MyIQCamBck-ve!

ItCudBWrseWhtIfSxWsFatning?

Soppy Text

H&K

Hugs and kisses.

H&KB

Hugs and kisses back.

H&KBB

Hugs and kisses back back.

H&KBBB

Hugs and kisses back back back.

H&KBBBB

Hugs and kisses back back back back.

OFCK - H&KBBBBB

Hugs and kisses back back back back back back – now stop sending me these stupid messages.

Emoticon Rhetoric

:-)—- \‹

> I really fancy you.

:-(—/‹

> I really fancy you but have had eight pints.

:-)=x‹

> I don't fancy you at all – I'm a eunuch.

(˅)   I work on a building site.

) , (Size doesn't matter.

UWot?!

) ! (	Size does matter.
) v (	I'm a virgin.
) x (	I'm an ex-virgin.
69	Let's have kinky sex.
96	Let's not have kinky sex, I'm not speaking to you.
99	Let's have a cone instead of kinky sex.
696969	Let's invite some others to have kinky sex.
:-)oO<	I'm pregnant.

what those text messages _really_ mean	

:-)o8<   It's twins!

;-#o< . - *
I've just vomited all over the floor.

;-)-SXY<   You have a very sexy body.

:+}-o'<   Your fly's undone.

?;+)   You are of questionable intelligence.

£:-(My head's pounding.

=:-(I'm having a bad hair day.

;-£   Put you money where your mouth is!

‹]:^)   Stop clowning around.

‹|:~,   You are an evil witch.

.-)   They used to call me Lucky.

:-@   You make me want to scream.

~:o   You're such a big baby.

:-}-8=‹   I'm delighted with the results of my silicone implants.

:-{-%=‹   I'm very unhappy with the results of my silicone implants.

what those text messages *really* mean

:-{}   Do you think I'm wearing too much lipstick?

(: (=   You're looking quite ghostly today.

:-o ^^;^^ Ouch! I've got my member caught in my zip.

$:-} B >   I'm a female prostitute.

$:-) : 8-   I'm a male prostitute.

:-) : 8-... I'm just taking a leak.

(:-) ?   I've had a sex change.

*:-} 8 8-   I'm a transvestite.

UWot?!

o:-)   I'm a little angel.

NO:-)   I'm no angel.

:-)~~~~~~ My boyfriend's got an awfully long tongue and it certainly has its advantages.

@:-}   Do you like my new hairdo?

;+)-8o{==== Is my mini-skirt too short?

;-(?)   Do you fancy a blowjob?

; &[}   Yes – I do work at a nuclear test site. How did you know?

Professionally Speaking

££CALLME££

I have charged you £200 for sending this message – Your Lawyer

GudNews-TestRsltsOK

You have only six months to live – Your Doctor.

BkSUCKS

Thanks for sending your manuscript. We have given it our full consideration (it has sat in a large pile on the junior editor's desk for eight weeks) but unfortunately it would not fit into our portfolio – Your Publisher.

FndUa3RmBunPrimLoc-VyDes+CHEAP

I've just found you a super three-bedroom bungalow in a prime location. This is a very desirable house and will therefore be double the price you can afford – Your Estate Agent

UrCmptrNds :100GbMem+PAS+12x8x32CDRW+TwnCams

I can't find the fault – Your Computer Consultant.

Nd2CanclUrDrvngLesn

I've not recovered from the nervous breakdown I had after your last lesson – Your Ex-Driving Instructor

PtThtCkeDwnNOW

> You may be miles away but I
> know exactly what you're up to –
> Your Dietician

BzzzPhnBzzz4BzzzApntmntBzzz

> Your six-monthly check-up is
> overdue – Your Dentist

UveGotMail

> Here's today's pile of junk mail
> and bills – Your Postman

Text of Yore

UWot?!

RmeoRmeoWhr4RtThoRmeo?
 – Shakespeare

HeyMrTmbrneManPlaASng4M-
ImNtSlpy+ThrIsNoPlceImGoin2
 – Bob Dylan

4IDntCre2Mch4£ – 4£CntByMeLuv
 – Lennon / McCartney

2ErIsHumn–2RlyFckUpRqrsACmptr
 – Anon

EvrythngShldBMde
AsSmplAsPsbleBtNtSmplr
 – Albert Einstein

what those text messages *really* mean

MnWnt2BAWmns1stLuv –
WmnLke2BAMnsLstRmnce
     – Oscar Wilde

LuvCnSumtmsBMgic-
BtMgicCnSumtmsJstBAnLusion
     – Javan

LuvIsThAnswrBtWhleURW8ng
4ThAnswrSxRasesSumPrtyGdQs
     – Woody Allen

ThNceThngAbtMstrb8n
IsThtUDntHve2DresUp4It.
     – Truman Capote

MunyWsXactlyLkeSx-
UThotOfNthngElsIfUDdntHve
It&ThotOfOthrThngsIfUDid
    – James Arthur Baldwin

OutsdeOfEvryThnWmn
IsAFatMnTryng2GtIn.
    – Katherine Whitehorn

2BInLuvIsMrly2BIn
APrptulSt8OfAnaesthesia
    – H. L. Mencken

IfURNot2LngIWlW8Hre4UalMyLife
    – Oscar Wilde

SxIsNtThAnswrSxIsThQ-YES
IsThAnswr
    – Swami X

IHvNotFaildIveJstFnd
10000WysThtWntWrk
— Thomas Edison

ThOnlyDfrnceBtwnSyncrnzed
Swmng&SxIsThtSyncrnzed
SwmngInvlvesLtsOfPeplIn
APoolNtMkngBdlyCntact
— Anon

OwadSumPowrThGiftieGie
Us2COurselsAsOthrsCUs
— Robert Burns

ThAnswr2ThGr8QofLf
ThUnvrs&Evrythng=42
— Douglas Adams

Communications is an Art

what those text messages *really* mean

:-)-<   *Portrait of an Extremely Fat*
                Woman
                by Lawrence Lowry

:o()   *Mona Lisa* by Leonardo da Vinci

:-)8=<   *Venus de Milo*

;+}=6<   *David* by Michaelangelo

! ? !   *The Three Graces*
                by Antonio Canova

Ý=> – - - - * *
                Wham! by Roy Lichtenstein

%^ , >   *Nude* by Pablo Picasso

UWot?!

[~QQ°] *Dead Cow in Formaldehyde*
by Damian Hurst

Oo°Oo *Blue Water Lilies*
by Claude Monet

@* ~@ *Starry Night*
by Vincent Van Gogh

;-)-8< oO~
Femme et Chat
by Joan Miro

><))))^;>
Self Portrait by John Bellany

HA..HA..

HAND Have a nice day.

HASH Have a super hour.

HAMM Have a memorable minute.

HATE Have a terrific evening.

HALT Have a lousy time.

HARM Have a rotten morning.

HARD Have a revolting day.

HAIR   Have an intolerable retirement.

HAIL   Have an irrational life.

HALB   Have a loathsome birthday.

HAXX   Have a fantastic sex life.

HA##   I don't give a shit what kind of
       day you have!

Prat-Text

DearSantaAFrndGavMeUrScret
NmberAndTldMeIfI
CaledUIdGetLotsOfPressies

> I'm a gullible little prat.

HiUDntKnoMe-
ICaldUrNmberAtRndom-
WilUGoOutWthMe?

> I'm a desperate little prat.

HlloMeIThotIWudJstSndMeAMssge

> I'm a lonely little prat.

FckWhyFckDidFckUFck
NotFckTurnFckUpFck2NiteFck?

> I'm an angry little prat.

Л = 3.1415926535897932384626
4338327950288419716939937510
58209749445923

I'm a boring little prat

ZModSrCrAp

I'm an enigmatic little prat.

Sun, Sand & Text

WshUWerHre

> I'm glad to get away from you for a while.

HvngAGr8tTme

> It's raining and there's nothing to do.

:-))8=‹   :-))=^‹

> We've found the nudist beach.

H ――― * ――→ C

> The hotel is just a stone's throw from the sea.

NtADrpOfRainAlWk

> It has snowed most days.

Stayn@a *** Hotl**

> The hotel we're staying at isn't 5-star; it's just shite.

116

what those text messages *really* mean

RlxngByPoolWthAG&T

> So busy here we can't find a place to sit and the queue for the bar is six-deep.

EvrythngsJstLikInThBrchur

> It looked crap in the brochure too.

Wow!ThsPlacIsAlveWthHotSxyBkniBabes

> Beach babes all around, yet as usual I just can't score.

GotASupaChepPckgeHolidy

> Sat for eighteen hours at the airport and the frigging hotel is still under construction.

MI5 Top Secret Encryptext

sghrhrzrdbqdsldrrzfdzantsylncrz
mcrgntkcmnsadqdzc

> Top secret – do not attempt to decode.

HKpp6wQ7dmB&rRMn$0LiR

> Help – I'm trapped deep behind enemy lines and my phone needs to be topped up.

@lk#99ZMODsRsHiTfyXM*urXfe)&in

> . . . and so I said to her 'that dress is far too tight' and she said . . .

WEAREOVERHEREYOU
WANKERSCOMEANDGETUS

> The great thing about this mobile
> is that you can send anything and
> the enemy hasn't a clue – oh shit,
> did I switch the encryption on?

SOS – SOS – SOS

> We've run out of ketchup. Can
> you airdrop a few bottles?

4-6-28-33-42-48

> Bert – here are this week's lottery
> numbers.

Thank God . . .

TGIF   Thank God It's Friday.

TGIODNF

Thank God It's One Day Nearer Friday.

TGIT   Thank God It's The-*day-before-*Friday.

TGIFT   Thank God It's Forever Today.

what those text messages *really* mean

TGIGOT
>Thank God I'm Going Out Tonight.

TGIDDY
>Thank God I Didn't Die Yesterday.

TGIVE
>Thank God I'm a Vivacious Egotist.

TGIRLS
>Thank God I Really Love Sex.

TGIWANK
>Thank God I Was A Normal Kid.

Just A Thought!

what those text messages *really* mean	
TOY	Thinking of You
TOS	Thinking of Someone else
TOB	Thinking of Boys
TOG	Thinking of Girls
TOE	Thinking of Ectoplasm
TOL	Thinking of Lust
TON	Thinking of Nothing
TOP	Thinking of Paranoia
TOT	Thinking of Telepathy
TOW	Thinking of Wanking
TOX	Thinking of something X-rated

Ambigunyms

what those text messages *really* mean

BUM Bring your Mother

BUM Blast your Mother

BUM Breasts Upset Me

BUM Breasts Uplift Me

BUM Boys Understand Me

BUM Boys Undress Me

BUM Bugger You Mate

BUM Bless You Mate

BUM Brilliantly Useful Men

BUM Bloody Useless Men

BUM Basically You're Mad

BUM Basically You're Magic

BUM Bananas Unite Menacingly

BUM Bananas Usually Masturbate

ARSE A Really Stupid Eegit

ARSE A Really Sensible Expert

ARSE Another Romantically Sweet
Encounter

ARSE Another Randy Sexual Encounter

ARSE Anal Retentive Supercilious
Extravert

ARSE Altruistic Responsible
Straightforward Earthling

ARSE Always Rancorously Seeking
Empathy

ARSE Aliens Released Stolen Earthling

ARSE Adult Rated Sexually Explicit

ARSE A Remarkably Sensational
Experience

**For the latest
humour books from
Summersdale,
check out**

www.summersdale.com